CW01390950

3 Minute Prayers

3 Minute Prayers

For the Evening

Linda Ottewell

kevin
mayhew

*For Gracie, who is such a joy
and a great blessing to us all.
Her laughter lights up the day.*

kevin
mayhew

First published in Great Britain in 2019 by Kevin Mayhew Ltd
Buxhall, Stowmarket, Suffolk IP14 3BW
Tel: +44 (0) 1449 737978 Fax: +44 (0) 1449 737834
E-mail: info@kevinmayhew.com

www.kevinmayhew.com

© Copyright 2019 Linda Ottewell

The right of Linda Ottewell to be identified as the author of this
work has been asserted by her in accordance with the Copyright,
Designs and Patents Act 1988. The publishers wish to thank all those
who have given their permission to reproduce copyright material in
this publication.

Unless stated otherwise, Scripture quotations are taken from
The New Revised Standard Version Bible: Anglicised Edition,
copyright © 1989, 1995, Division of Christian Education of the
National Council of the Churches of Christ in the United States of
America. Used by permission. All rights reserved.

Scripture quotations are also from The Holy Bible, New International
Version® Anglicised, NIV®, copyright © 1979, 1984, 2011 by Biblica
Inc.®. Used by permission. All rights reserved worldwide.

All rights reserved. No part of this publication may be reproduced,
stored in a retrieval system, or transmitted, in any form or by
any means, electronic, mechanical, photocopying, recording, or
otherwise, without the prior written permission of the publisher.

9 8 7 6 5 4 3 2 1 0

ISBN 978 1 84867 986 3
Catalogue No. 1501607

Cover design by Rob Mortonson
© Image used under licence from Shutterstock Inc.
Typeset by Angela Selfe

Printed and bound in Great Britain

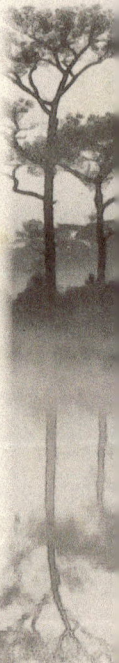

Contents

SECTION 1

God's love for us, his children

SECTION 2

Embracing God's love

SECTION 3

Staying faithful and trusting God

SECTION 4

Serving God and others

SECTION 5

Becoming more like Jesus

SECTION 6

Words of encouragement

About the author

Based in Suffolk since 1992, Linda has an academic background in modern languages and taught English as a Foreign Language before joining Kevin Mayhew Ltd in 2000 as a proofreader and editor of books and music.

Outside work, Linda is a long-standing member of her local parish church, where she plays the clarinet in the music group, is part of the prayer ministry team and regularly writes and leads intercessions in the Sunday morning services.

Afflicted with an incurable love of studying, in recent years Linda has completed theology and vocation courses by distance learning from St John's Theological College in Nottingham, and a certificate in counselling skills for pastoral care.

Music, reading and handicrafts are firm hobbies, while she can bore for England on the joys of keeping house rabbits and the benefits of Pilates as a means of exercise and relaxation!

Creative writing has been an enduring pastime and Linda is delighted to have prepared and presented her own work for publication, after many years of reading and correcting other authors' proofs.

Introduction

**Draw near to God,
and he will draw near to you.**

James 4:8

Whatever kind of day you've had, it's always good to spend time in God's company as the evening closes in and you prepare for rest and sleep.

This book of short devotions will help you to reflect on your day, not pulling it apart and conducting a self-critical 'post mortem' but considering where God has been with you in the everyday routine. Guided by the Holy Spirit, it's an opportunity to unwind, relax and let go of the strains and stresses of the day, to focus on God's bigger picture, round off the day, bring it to a good conclusion and look ahead to tomorrow.

Starting with the words 'God is love', the devotions examine the nature of God's love for us, his children. Embracing a deeper sense of our Father God's love, how do we then respond to his never-failing love and care? Our commitment will surely be to remain faithful and trusting, with a desire to serve God and others. As our love for God grows, so we are changed to become more like Jesus.

You may only have a few minutes to spare but that's fine. Each meditation begins with a Bible verse, followed by a brief reflection. This is finished off with a few questions or suggestions for you to ponder, then a sentence or two of prayer to conclude.

These evening prayers are meant to encourage a deeper understanding of God's love and inspire a closer walk with our wonderful God. As you read and reflect, my hope is that you will be blessed and inspired, refreshed and renewed.

Let my prayer be counted as incense before you,
and the lifting up of my hands
as an evening sacrifice.

Psalm 141:2

God's love for us, his children

1

✿

God is love

**God is love, and those who abide in love
abide in God, and God abides in them.**

1 John 4:16

❧

REFLECTION

'God is love.' Three familiar words that you may have
often sung in a hymn or worship chorus. But what
does this concise statement mean and what are its
implications? The writer says that love is not only a
quality that God has, rather God's essence is love. It's
not only that God loves, but that he is love and his
nature is to love. God is the source of all love and our
understanding of love comes from him.

Divine love is unconditional and doesn't depend on
whether its object is worthy to be loved. We can't earn
God's love and don't deserve it. God showed his love
by sending Jesus to the world to be our Saviour. Such
love in action was entirely for our benefit, with the
initiative coming solely from God and not dependent
on whether we choose to love him in return. Jesus,
love incarnate, in his act of supreme self-sacrifice

revealed the nature of divine love, so that all people might know God. Without that saving love, there could be no hope for the world. Love was the only way that God's just and righteous anger could be satisfied, bringing us forgiveness and reconciliation with him, and was only achieved at infinite cost to the One who loves.

PONDER

Reflect on the words: 'God is love.'
What is their impact on you?

When and how have you been aware of
God's love during the day?

How can you be more open to God's Holy Spirit,
who helps you to love God and others?

PRAYER

Father, Son and Holy Spirit,
divine Trinity of love,
surround and enfold me, I pray,
and grant me a better understanding
of the nature
of your love for me.

2

Children of God

**See what great love the Father has lavished on us,
that we should be called children of God!
And that is what we are!**

1 John 3:1 (NIV)

REFLECTION

God's love for us is so overwhelming that it should stop us in our tracks and fill us with wonder. This verse captures the writer's amazement at the abundance of this freely-given love. Motivated by his limitless and unconditional love, God draws us to himself, adopting us into his family and according us the full rights and privileges of a child of God. He is the perfect Father who understands all our needs, will never let us down and always acts in our best interests.

It may be hard to accept God's unconditional love. Instead, we may try to prove ourselves good enough by what we do. We are saved to serve but saved by grace alone. Perhaps we should pause from time to time and consider how much of what we are busy doing is a response to our love for God. How much is it, in fact, an attempt to impress and prove ourselves to God and other people? Our relationship with God is crucial, for who we are in relation to him is far more important than what we do. Our security comes from understanding that our identity as a child of God has been given by grace alone and doesn't depend on anything we do.

PONDER

You are a dearly-loved child of God: let that sink down into the depth of your being.

Do you feel secure in God's unconditional love and acceptance or do you feel the need to prove yourself?

Looking back over your day, has anything you have done been motivated by a desire to impress or because of group pressure, the need to belong?

PRAYER

Abba Father, I come to you,
a child in your presence,
and rejoice that you love me
with an everlasting love
that will never let me go or fail me.
Thank you for your tender loving-kindness to me.

3

❧

The Father's Song

The Lord your God is with you,
he is mighty to save.
He will take great delight in you,
he will quiet you with his love,
he will rejoice over you with singing.

Zephaniah 3:17 (NIV)

🌿

REFLECTION

This verse from Zephaniah, one of the more obscure
Old Testament prophets, is often quoted in isolation
and taken to be a direct promise for us as Christians.
To the extent that we sincerely seek God and desire
to draw closer to him, trust and faithfully follow him,
we can draw parallels between the faithful remnant
that Zephaniah wrote of and ourselves as followers of
God in the twenty-first century.

Imagine that God is speaking the words of this verse to
you personally. He is your mighty Saviour and Lord and
is with you in every circumstance of life. He takes great
delight in you, stilling you with his love. Joyfully he sings
over you, with a song tailor-made for you alone. God's

words speak of his acceptance of you, his great mercy and love, provision and protection. By God's good grace you can find in him your identity and security, and all your needs are met. The Father treasures you, his child, and is concerned about every detail of your life.

God's love is affirming and positive; he wants to encourage and reassure us, to make us feel good about ourselves. It's up to us to draw near and listen to him and be open to all he wants to say to us.

PONDER

Have you been aware of God speaking to you today, or singing over you?

Consider what God's song is like for you. Is it loud and booming, making the earth shake or is it tender and soft, a lullaby to calm and quieten, to soothe your soul? Can you fully appreciate the harmony and beauty of God's song to you?

Has anything in your day blocked God's voice?

PRAYER

Father God, quieten my heart and mind that
I may listen, not to the clamour of this busy
world, constantly pressing for attention,
but to your unique love song for me.

❦

All God's love

**I pray that you may have the power
to comprehend, with all the saints,
what is the breadth and length and height
and depth, and to know the love of Christ
that surpasses knowledge, so that you may
be filled with all the fullness of God.**

Ephesians 3:18, 19

🌿

REFLECTION

These verses are part of a longer prayer by Paul for the Christians in the Ephesus Church. In an ever-changing world, God's love proves to be constant, faithful and never-failing. The love of God is unique to each of his beloved children, intricate and personal. All God's love is given to each one of us, completely and perfectly. St Augustine wrote that 'God loves each of us, as if there was only one of us to love.' How wonderful that God chooses to give us all his love, not simply a little bit. It's the opposite of a huge cake that's divided up into slices, a small piece for you, or a few crumbs here and there. We are offered the whole cake – all God's love, freely given, although we have done nothing to deserve it.

Even before we were born, before we had the opportunity to do anything, whether good or bad, God loved us. He delights in us as part of his marvellous creation and loves us 'just as we are'. Nothing can change the way God loves us and nothing can ever separate us from this love. Even if we were the only person who needed Christ's sacrifice, he would still have gone to the cross to bring us salvation and eternal life.

PONDER

Have you felt safe and secure in God's all-sufficient love throughout the day?

Are you confident of God's never-changing, unconditional love, acceptance and approval?

Rest in God's presence and let his love enfold you.

PRAYER

Heavenly Father, as the roots of my faith
grow ever deeper into you, may I know the
full extent of your love for me and be filled
to overflowing with all the fullness of God.

❀

The Servant King

Then he poured water into a basin and began to wash the disciples' feet and to wipe them with the towel that was tied around him.

John 13:5

🌿

REFLECTION

It was during the Last Supper, on the evening before his death, that Jesus carried out this humble act for his disciples, a lowly task usually performed by a servant. He was setting his disciples an example to follow but also showing them how much he loved them. It could well be that all the disciples felt totally unworthy of such an action by their Lord and teacher, but we only have an account of Peter's reaction. He was adamant at first that Jesus would never wash his feet. Was it a mixture of confusion, not feeling good enough that Jesus should want to do this for him, or his pride, as he tried to tell Jesus what he should and shouldn't do? Jesus insisted, however, and the washing of the disciples' feet became a symbolic precursor to the following day, when Jesus' death on the cross would wash away the sins of the world, not with water but by his own blood, and so reveal the full extent of his sacrificial love.

The washing of the disciples' feet shows how we, too, can approach our heavenly Father exactly as we are, without reproach, experience his unconditional love and acceptance, and be washed clean.

PONDER

Imagine that Jesus, the Servant King, kneels to wash *your* feet. How do you respond? Like Peter? Do you wish you'd had a wash first?

How does Jesus wash your feet? Grudgingly, with distaste, reproaching you for not keeping them cleaner? Or gently, tenderly, with compassion, and a smile on his face?

Looking back over your day, have there been moments when have you felt completely accepted and loved by God?

PRAYER

Lord God, however unworthy I feel in approaching you, may I receive gratefully your love and acceptance, and your cleansing touch.

Perfectly known
and loved by God

O Lord, you have searched me and known me.
You know when I sit down and when I rise up;
    you discern my thoughts from far away.
You search out my path and my lying down,
    and are acquainted with all my ways.
    Even before a word is on my tongue,
    O Lord, you know it completely.

Psalm 139:1-4

REFLECTION

In this well-loved psalm, we see a marvellous picture
of our relationship with our heavenly Father. God is
all-knowing, everywhere present and all-powerful; his
knowledge and understanding of us is perfect. All our
thoughts, words and actions are open before him, yet
he still accepts and loves us unconditionally.

With God there can be no pretence or hiding; every
detail of our life is known to him and we are invited
to be completely honest in his presence, holding

nothing back. We may adopt the less than honest brave face with other people and be able to fool them (I'm fine, really . . .) but it's impossible to hide from God how we're feeling. We come into God's presence exactly as we are. Any denial on our part will only hinder a closer walk with him. God is watching over us in love, not like a menacing Big Brother figure or an old-fashioned schoolmaster, waiting to punish us if we should step out of line. We have nothing to fear, for we are loved, cherished and precious to God and he is interested in every part of our lives – body, mind and emotions.

PONDER

Visualise your life as a house. Are some rooms shut or locked to keep God out?

What would it take to open those doors and let God in? Are you willing to do so?

Tell God how you feel right now and share with him all that's on your heart.

PRAYER

Thank you, heavenly Father, that you know me through and through. Enfold me in your perfect, life-affirming love, I pray.

❧

The power of God's love

I am convinced that neither death, nor life, nor angels, nor rulers, nor things present, nor things to come, nor powers, nor height, nor depth, nor anything else in all creation, will be able to separate us from the love of God in Christ Jesus our Lord.

Romans 8:38, 39

REFLECTION

Paul presents an exhaustive list of the different ways God's love might be thwarted and concludes that it's impossible to get beyond God's loving reach. There is nothing stronger than God's love. Diamonds, much-prized stones of pure carbon, are the hardest naturally-occurring substance we know. God's precious love is like a many-faceted diamond, bringing light and life to our dark world. In Jesus we see God's loving power in action. The Gospels record many instances of him exercising his divine power to forgive people their sins, and to heal body, mind and spirit. Ultimately, Jesus overcame the power of sin and death itself.

Whatever happens to you in this life, nothing can ever separate you from the love of God. Even if all else fails, the unbreakable lifeline of God's all-powerful love will remain, like an umbilical cord connecting you to him. The promise of God's love to sustain and keep us is wonderfully comforting, particularly in times of trouble. In life's storms, when life is at its most challenging, we can feel safe and totally secure in God's all-powerful love.

PONDER

Picture a sparkling diamond and reflect on God's all-powerful love for you.

How have you, or the people you've met today, been sustained by God's love?

Ask for more opportunities to share God's love, especially with those going through difficult times.

PRAYER

Precious Lord, I draw strength from your
wonderful promise to be with me by the
loving power of your indwelling Holy Spirit,
sustaining and leading me on,
in every circumstance of life.

❀

God's loving protection through the night

**I will both lie down and sleep in peace;
for you alone, O Lord,
make me lie down in safety.**

Psalm 4:8

🌿

REFLECTION

David's confidence, trust and faith in his Lord shine through this verse. Even in times of fear and trouble, David is sure of God's protection and he can sleep soundly, safe and secure in God's love.

You may have had a long, trying day, and are relieved it's finally coming to an end. Even if you are feeling unsettled, fearful, isolated, lonely or vulnerable, you are not alone, because God is with you, watching over you and protecting you. Ask him for restful sleep. Picture yourself as a small child, snuggling down for the night in a warm, cosy bed. You can feel safe and secure, comfortable and contented, free from care and anxiety. In the stillness and quiet you can be calm, with nothing to fear. This is truly a good place to rest.

Your heavenly Father longs to bless you with his inner peace, that brings release from fear and worry. His peace of heart and mind goes beyond our understanding, to produce total well-being. At the end of his mission on earth, Jesus spoke words of comfort to his disciples: 'Peace I leave with you; my peace I give to you. I do not give to you as the world gives. Do not let your hearts be troubled, and do not let them be afraid' (John 14:27).

PONDER

Do you tend to take your worries to bed with you and find yourself so tense and wound up that you can't sleep easily?

Are you anxious or fearful about something right now?

Can you trust God fully with your safety and security?

PRAYER

Steadfast, loving God, let me feel safe
in your never-failing care and protection.
Surround me with your perfect peace
this night, I pray.

Embracing God's love

1

&

Responding to God's love

We love because he first loved us.

1 John 4:19

REFLECTION

Love began with God and all love comes ultimately from him. Without his love, there would be no love in our world and no world, in fact, for God's creative activity derives from his nature, which is love. Our capacity to love is part of being made in the image of God and is only possible because of God's love in the first place. Love is the greatest gift that we receive from God, who is the source of all human love. When we respond to his initiative, the Holy Spirit gives us the power to love through his indwelling in our hearts, as he makes us more like Jesus.

The poster on my office wall has the words: 'We learn to love, not by being told to love but by being loved.' The proof of any claim we make to love God is borne out by how we also love others, which we are commanded to do by God, and how we allow God to love others through us. Exactly what kind of love are we considering here? It's much more than a feeling, it's a decision to love, and love in action. The kind of love that is based on those wonderful verses from 1 Corinthians 13, the essential motivation, without which the spiritual gifts that Paul goes on to detail in the following chapter have no value. 'Follow the way of love,' he tells his readers.

PONDER

Before God made you, he loved you with an everlasting love. How do you respond to such love?

Looking back over the day, have you had God-given opportunities to love others as you have been loved by God?

How do you love the people that you don't particularly like, who perhaps rub you up the wrong way?

PRAYER

Thank you, Father God, for your gift
of love to me. May I learn to love you
and those around me with the love
that you are growing in me.

2

❀

First in my heart

Whom have I in heaven but you?
And there is nothing on earth
that I desire other than you.

Psalm 73:25

🌿

REFLECTION

For the Psalmist, nothing is more important in his life than God. He desires God above all other things: God is first in his heart. Many people desire wealth and status, material possessions, and other attractive but temporary things of this world. To some extent they can bring satisfaction and security, happiness and fulfilment but remain, by definition, finite. We will never be totally fulfilled or happy with what the world can offer. As a test of our devotion to God, we should consider whether our desires are directed to his kingdom and his love or directed to our personal kingdom of comfort, wealth, status and success.

In his Sermon on the Mount, Jesus warned against storing up treasures on earth, which may gleam and glitter for a while, but threaten to preoccupy us, becoming the centre of our life instead of God. Jesus told his followers to store up lasting treasures in heaven instead. Whatever we treasure the most, where our heart is, will determine how we live (Matthew 6:19-21). We are to love and value lasting treasures that money can't buy, such as God's love and peace, more than the things which only satisfy our passing desires.

PONDER

Consider the difference between what you wanted during the day and what you truly needed.

Where does your treasure lie?

Who or what is your heart's desire?

PRAYER

Dear Lord, help me to understand
the difference between what I desire
and what I really need,
for I know that whatever
I treasure the most,
where my heart is,
will determine how I live.

3

❀

Freedom in the love of God

**So if the Son makes you free,
you will be free indeed.**

John 8:36

🌿

REFLECTION

God's love in Jesus releases us from sin, anxiety and fear, for Jesus alone is the One who makes known the truth that can set people free. The freedom Christ offers is personal, eternal and a gift from God, nothing we can earn. What does it mean to be free and what is true freedom? We are released from the power of sin to live as God wants us to live, to become the person God wants us to be. We have free will to choose to love God, who is committed to setting people free, always ready to give a fresh start, and who desires a loving response from us. If we allow God's Spirit of love to dwell within us, his freedom can make us whole. We are free to enjoy new opportunities and new ways of being, to experience God's peace and life in all its fullness, as promised by Jesus.

Many people are searching for true freedom – from feelings such as guilt, regret, and hopelessness, but they are looking in the wrong places. They hope to achieve freedom and satisfaction through reliance on such things as material wealth, ambition, self-indulgence, or addictions to alcohol or drugs. However, they end up being slaves to the very things they hoped would bring them freedom.

PONDER

Do you feel enslaved to anything in your life? How could you break its power over you?

Consider what it cost Jesus to buy your freedom. What is your response to the price he paid?

Sin isn't a popular word these days. How could you convey God's message using words a non-churchgoer might understand better?

PRAYER

Lord Jesus, thank you for the price
you paid to buy my freedom.

❦

4

Eyes fixed on God

**So Peter got out of the boat, started walking
on the water, and came towards Jesus.
But when he noticed the strong wind,
he became frightened, and beginning
to sink, he cried out, 'Lord, save me!'**

Matthew 14:29, 30

🌿

REFLECTION

Matthew 14:25-33 relates how Jesus walked on the
water towards his disciples who were in a boat that was
being buffeted by the waves. When Peter realised it
was Jesus, he wanted to walk to him on the water. Jesus
invited Peter to come to him and, initially fired up
with enthusiasm and with his eyes fixed on Jesus, Peter
had no doubt that he could defy gravity. However,
when Peter took his eyes off Jesus and focused on
the wind instead, his fears overwhelmed him, and he
began to sink, crying out to Jesus for help in panic and
desperation. Jesus chided Peter for his lack of faith;
together they climbed into the boat and the wind
immediately died down – it had lost its power over Peter.

Substitute the wind and waves for whatever problems or setbacks we may be confronting. Distracted by the circumstances which are demanding attention, it's all too easy to lose a sense of perspective, instead of keeping our eyes fixed on God and his love, leaving us feeling out of our depth and sinking. Once we call out to God for help, readjust our focus, trust his never-failing love and promises, and depend on his strength, then we can feel safe and secure with our Lord once more.

PONDER

Who do you turn to for help during the day?
Is God your first or last resort?

What about those times when God seems distant or absent?

In difficult times, are you able to trust God's loving care and promises, even if you haven't much conviction of their truth?

PRAYER

Lord God, help me to depend on your
never-failing love and faithful promises,
and to focus on you alone.

❧

5

Searching and finding

'The kingdom of heaven is like treasure
hidden in a field, which someone found
and hid; then in his joy, he goes and sells
all that he has and buys that field.
'Again, the kingdom of God is like a
merchant in search of fine pearls; on
finding one pearl of great value, he went
and sold all that he had and bought it.'

Matthew 13:44, 45

🌿

REFLECTION

Jesus spoke of searching for what is truly important
in life and finding it. Using images his disciples could
understand, he taught them about God's kingdom
of love. The message was clear: God's kingdom is of
all-surpassing value and to possess it, we should be
willing to give up everything. The treasure in the
field was of such immense value that when the man
found it, he was overwhelmed with joy. Realising that
everything he already had paled into insignificance by
comparison, he simply had to have that treasure. The

field was costly, taking all that he had, but the treasure itself came free.

So it is with God's kingdom of love. We may have searched long and hard for what is truly important in life and when we find it, the cost may be great in terms of letting go of whatever we consider valuable and cling to. If we truly believe that God's kingdom of love is of supreme importance, to be accepted as a gift, we will receive the kingdom with joy and recognise that nothing else in life is more important. The treasures of this world will loosen their grip on us.

PONDER

How important to you is the kingdom of God's love?

What has the search for God's kingdom cost you and how easy is it to let go of the things you cling to?

Are you able to receive God's kingdom each day with joy, recognising that nothing else in life is of greater value?

PRAYER

Precious God, my all-surpassing treasure, fill me with love and joy and be all in all to me.

6

✤

Resting in God's love

**'Come with me by yourselves to a
quiet place and get some rest.'**

Mark 6:31 (NIV)

🌿

REFLECTION

Jesus had sent out his twelve disciples in pairs on their
third preaching tour in Galilee. On their return they
needed a time of rest and renewal alone with Jesus
to recharge their batteries and recover, physically
and spiritually.

For Christians, it's a question of establishing a proper
God-centred balance to our lives. Work, important
as it is, can take up a great deal of our energy and
attention, and even become all-consuming. There can
be a tendency to focus on 'doing' – keeping busy (too
busy?) in God's service. If we find ourselves without
enough rest and spiritual refreshment, over-scheduled
with meetings and good works and neglecting our
overall well-being, something is very wrong. God's
call is to slow down, stop, relax and find our rest and
refreshment in him. We need that 'quiet place', a time

of calm and stillness to engage in reflective, seeking and waiting prayer. Unless we spend enough time 'being', our 'doing' will become aimless, directionless and unfruitful. God offers the opportunity to find a resting-place with him, amidst the apparent mayhem of daily life.

PONDER

Do you think your day has been balanced?

Have you excluded God from certain parts of your day?

How do you regard the Sabbath, the day of the week given by God for our benefit, so we can rest and recover, a time for reflection and worship?

PRAYER

Lord, may I welcome your love
into my life each day.
May I rest in your love,
listen and respond
to your Spirit within me.

✻

7

Abiding in God's love

'I am the vine, you are the branches. Those who abide in me and I in them bear much fruit, because apart from me you can do nothing.'

John 15:5

🌿

REFLECTION

On the evening before his death, Jesus prepared his disciples for what lay ahead by teaching them more about their calling and mission, underlining their dependence on him. Only by abiding, remaining and living in relationship with Jesus, the true vine, would their efforts be fruitful.

God the Father is the gardener, the vine-grower, who has grafted us into Jesus, the true vine. We are united with Christ by faith, a faith that comes from God and depends on his grace. This life-giving connection with Christ must be continuous – we are called to keep on trusting and to persevere in our faith. Abiding involves our submission, obedience, commitment, and dependence on God, allowing his words and his love to dwell in us. We receive life and power from Jesus, the true vine and without him we, the vine branch, would be useless. It is Christ's work through us that will bear fruit, for without him our efforts are in vain. Fruitfulness is to become more like Jesus, transformed in our character and to grow the fruit of the Spirit in us. Fruitfulness also lies in our mission to fulfil Christ's command to continue the work he began while on earth.

PONDER

Reflect on the image of the vine. What kind of branch are you?

Which areas of the fruit of the Spirit need more work in your life?

How have you been obedient to Christ's call to mission today?

PRAYER

May Christ the vine dwell in my heart, I pray.
Strengthen my faith and deepen my love,
that I may bear much fruit.

❀

8

Misconceptions

There is no fear in love, but perfect love casts out fear; for fear has to do with punishment.

1 John 4:18

🌿

REFLECTION

We may have false ideas about God's love and intentions that are based on our upbringing, transferring to God our experience of parenthood, especially our father figure. God chooses and calls us, we have been taught. We may be anxious about embracing God's love and committing ourselves wholeheartedly to him in case he demands too much of us. God has a purpose and a plan for our lives, we are told. What if we step outside his will? We worry about not being willing or good enough for what God has in store, that we will fail to live up to his exacting standards and expectations. The focus is on our own efforts, our need to be a better person and witness, to do more for God, make more progress in our spiritual life. We fear God's judgement and punishment every time we fail, waiting for something bad to happen to us. All of which may lead to discouragement or holding back, and perhaps the temptation to give up altogether.

It's time to learn what God is really like, to focus on his loving-kindness, his love without measure, and fully believe and trust his word and promises. To be confident that we are accepted and loved by God; we are his precious children.

PONDER

Do you find it hard to believe that God accepts and loves you, not in spite of who you are but because of who you are?

Do you harbour false notions about God's love and his intentions for you, perhaps based on your past?

Rest in God and enjoy peace and freedom in his perfect love that casts out fear.

PRAYER

Father God, when I find it difficult to believe that you accept me, exactly as I am, and you delight in me, help me to set aside my fears and anxieties and rest in your perfect love.

Staying faithful and trusting God

1

❧

A childlike trust
and faith

**'Truly I tell you, whoever does not
receive the kingdom of God as a
little child will never enter it.'**

Mark 10:15

REFLECTION

The disciples criticised people for bringing little
children to Jesus. Rebuking his disciples for their
attitude, Jesus proceeded to take the children in
his arms, lay his hands on them and bless them.
In Jesus' day children had little status or influence
but Jesus overturned the social values of the time,
affirming the children and telling people that the
kingdom of God belongs to those who receive it as a
gift, not by trying to earn it with their own efforts or
because they believe themselves entitled.

Words we associate with children include trusting,
open and receptive, dependent, unpretentious, innocent
and unsophisticated, less inhibited. Consider what it

means to come to God as a child. We can't undo those experiences of life that may have led to a world-weary cynicism, but we can change our attitude. We can humble ourselves before God, stop trying to make our faith too complicated, and open our hearts more fully to him. We should learn to accept that we can't understand everything – that's where faith comes in. It might be enough simply to know that God loves us and forgives us.

PONDER

Picture yourself as one of the children brought to Jesus that day. Jesus gently takes you in his arms, lays his hands on you and blesses you. What do you see when you look into his eyes?

How do you respond? Is it a scene of warmth, great laughter and joy for you or are other emotions coming to the fore?

Looking back over your day, has there been anything to hinder a childlike faith and trust on your part?

PRAYER

Heavenly Father, teach me how to lay down unhelpful attitudes of pride and self-sufficiency and let me come to you more like a child, with an open heart and mind, ready to trust and love you.

2

❧

Commitment

**Where you go, I will go,
and where you stay I will stay.**

Ruth 1:16 (NIV)

❧

REFLECTION

Ruth showed her devotion, loyalty and love for her mother-in-law, Naomi, by her willingness to stay with her. Ruth was prepared to give up a great deal in her commitment to care for Naomi. Consequently, Ruth's life changed in a way that she could never have imagined. She was King David's great-grandmother and an ancestor of Christ himself.

In response to God's love, we are invited to put our whole trust and faith in his loving purposes for our life. It's a costly commitment, with a pledge like the promise made by Ruth – to go and do whatever God wants us to do, wherever it may take us. Such a total, unconditional commitment may take a lifetime to learn and we cannot hope to succeed without God's help. Throughout the Bible there are accounts of God calling people, as they were, with all their strengths and weaknesses, and making them fit for his purpose. Commitment involves every aspect of life, and might mean hard times, as well as happiness and joy. The key is to offer our whole self in submission to God's will and in wholehearted commitment to his service. It has been said that unless Jesus Christ is Lord of all our life, then he is not Lord at all.

PONDER

Do you hesitate to commit yourself more fully to God, afraid of what he may ask you to do or where he may lead you?

Are you unwilling to give up some things in your life in order to walk more closely with God?

Can you entrust yourself wholeheartedly to God's care?

PRAYER

Lord God, help me to commit to you
all that I am and all that I do.
That I may go forward with you,
trusting in your loving purposes
for my life.

3

The trials of life

My brothers and sisters, whenever you face trials of any kind, consider it nothing but joy, because you know that the testing of your faith produces endurance; and let endurance have its full effect, so that you may be mature and complete, lacking in nothing.

James 1:2-4

REFLECTION

There is a well-known story that tells of a man watching a butterfly as it struggled for hours to emerge from a little hole in its cocoon. When the butterfly seemed to stop making any progress, the man tried to help by opening up the cocoon with a small pair of scissors. The butterfly was then easily free but had a tiny, withered body and shrivelled wings, and was unable to fly. The long struggle was crucial and involved forcing fluid from its body into its wings, so that it could fly. The butterfly's growth remained stunted and it never achieved its full potential, strength and beauty.

Sometimes struggles in life are exactly what we need to make us strong, resilient and able to persevere. James recognises it will be *when* we face difficulties, not *if* but he isn't saying we should put on a fixed grin and pretend all is well, that we're happy and thankful to be suffering trials and difficulties. Rather, we should adopt a positive outlook because of how the trials in life can be times of growth, making us 'mature and complete', the people God wants us to be, better able to serve him and others. God will never abandon us during such times but promises to be with us, to strengthen us and help us to endure.

PONDER

If you are going through a tough time, are you able to 'consider it nothing but joy' or do the words have a hollow ring to them? Be honest.

Look back to previous times of trial and recall how God helped you on those occasions.

In the course of your day, have you been able to be alongside someone who is going through a hard time?

PRAYER

Dear Lord, as I think about the butterfly's stunted growth, let me trust you when problems and trials come along, that I may achieve my full potential, strength and beauty in you.

❀

4

The potter
and the clay

**Yet, O Lord, you are our Father;
we are the clay, and you are our potter;
we are all the work of your hand.**

Isaiah 64:8

REFLECTION

A skilled potter moulds the lump of raw clay, working it to remove impurities, flaws and defects, gradually shaping and reshaping it until satisfied with the finished product. The clay is then baked hard, painted and glazed, and is ready to be used for whatever purpose the potter has in mind.

It takes faith and trust to allow God to be like the potter, to take us, like the clay, and make us into the person he intends us to be, and we have the choice to yield or to resist. We need to be open to God, placing ourselves in his hands, willing to be changed, letting him shape and mould us. We must be malleable, allowing God to work on our lives and transform us, removing whatever has no place there. God, the divine potter, wants to be Sovereign Lord of our lives, the expression of his creativity, working in us to make something beautiful and useful. He sees our potential and though we may at times hinder his purposes, he perseveres. His skill and power can make something of us far beyond what we dare imagine or deserve. As Paul tells the believers at Philippi: 'The one who began a good work among you will bring it to completion by the day of Jesus Christ' (Philippians 1:6).

PONDER

Reflect on the image of God the divine potter, gradually and skilfully transforming your life.

Have there been times recently when you have resisted God?

How could you align your will more closely to God's loving purposes for you?

PRAYER

Sovereign Lord, you have begun
a good work in me and I pray
you will persevere until it is complete.
Forgive me when I hinder your progress.

5

❧

Change and uncertainty

**Ship your grain across the sea;
after many days you may receive a return.**

Ecclesiastes 11:1 (NIV)

REFLECTION

This verse advocates being adventurous and taking a risk, not always playing it safe and missing opportunities as a result. As the writer goes on to say, it's a mistake to wait until the conditions are perfect before deciding to do something, for that will never happen. We can't live our lives thinking about what might have been if we'd been more courageous and stepped out in faith with God, strong in his strength, instead of timidly taking the safe option. Do we choose risky living or apparent security, steering a steady course, keeping to familiar paths, self-protection and comfort?

If we are willing to step out and trust him, God will lead us in new directions, into uncharted waters, taking us ever deeper, stretching and growing our faith. He wants us to be open to change, take a calculated risk, and embrace what he intends for us, to be at peace upon the open sea. Change may be painful and involve seeing ourselves and the world around us in a different, more honest way. It may mean shedding unnecessary baggage on the journey. We will need to increase our vision and expectation of what God can do.

PONDER

Have there been times recently when God has been nudging you in a new direction?

If God is calling you to make a change, what are you most afraid of leaving behind?

Are you able to welcome and embrace change and growth?

PRAYER

Let me live with uncertainty as with a friend;
to feel certain means feeling secure;
to feel secure is unreal, a delusion of self.

(St Anselm)

✿

6

Trust in God's guidance

Thus says the Lord:
Stand at the crossroads, and look,
and ask for the ancient paths,
where the good way lies;
and walk in it and find rest for your souls.

Jeremiah 6:16

REFLECTION

Jeremiah speaks about choosing the right way, God's way, but sadly the people being addressed rejected God's path and followed their own instincts instead.

Throughout the course of our life, God will guide, teach and advise us, but we need to pay attention to what he's saying and remain obedient to his will, and not only when his way suits us. It may take a lifetime to learn such obedience, to accept that God's way is the best and is tailor-made for each one of us. We are given choices, the freedom to accept God's will or to reject it, but his plan for our life isn't so rigid that it's a strict blueprint that must be followed to the last letter. There is a conflict between what we believe is best and being willing to follow the path God sets out before us, embracing his guidance. The more time we spend in God's presence, the more we will recognise his voice and understand his guidance and teaching. We will increasingly learn to turn to God for help, strength and support along the way. God will never leave us alone but will always be with us and will provide all the resources we need to follow his way.

PONDER

Are you at a crossroads in your life, wondering where you will go from here?

Will you have to leave anything behind at this crossroads in order to move on?

Look back at where you've come from, the road travelled so far and how God has guided you.

PRAYER

Lord, my vision is limited but you see the whole of my life's journey, from beginning to end. May I always trust your guidance and follow the way you lead me.

❀

7

In times of fear and anxiety

Suddenly a furious storm came up on the lake, so that the waves swept over the boat. But Jesus was sleeping. The disciples went and woke him, saying, 'Lord, save us! We're going to drown.'

Matthew 8:24, 25 (NIV)

🌿

REFLECTION

A sudden storm on the Sea of Galilee caused the disciples to panic. Among them were experienced fishermen sailing on familiar waters, so the danger must have been acute for them to respond in such a way. As the waves threatened to swamp the boat and sink it, the disciples' entire focus was quite naturally on the problem. Unbelievably, Jesus was still fast asleep! By crying out to him the disciples were acknowledging that Jesus was the solution to their fears and anxiety, but how confident were they of his power to act? Jesus calmed the storm and the disciples' reaction was telling. Although they had seen previous miracles, they were absolutely amazed.

Being a Christian offers no exemption from the storms of life. We are promised God's presence with us in the storm, just as Jesus was with his disciples in the boat. But maybe there's an experience that causes fear and anxiety and we feel that God can't or won't help, as symbolised by Jesus sleeping. It's easy to conclude that God isn't in control of what we're going through if nothing seems to change, or if things get even worse. Looking back at how God has helped you in the past can give a better perspective on any present problems and encourage you to keep going.

PONDER

Can you look back at times when God has been at work in your life, but you haven't realised it till later?

Do you believe that God has everything in hand? Can you trust him completely with your welfare?

Where do you turn in a crisis? Is God your first or last resort?

PRAYER

Thank you, Lord, that you are almighty and in control of every situation in life that I face, even if it's not apparent at the time. Help me to remember this and put my faith and trust in you.

8

❀

Obedience

**Jesus said to Simon, 'Put out into the deep
water and let down your nets for a catch.'
Simon answered, 'Master, we have worked
all night long but have caught nothing.
Yet if you say so, I will let down the nets.'**

Luke 5:4, 5

🌿

REFLECTION

Quite understandably, Simon might have reacted
negatively to Jesus' instruction, thinking, 'Who's the
experienced fisherman here, me or Jesus?' However,
he listened to Jesus, followed his advice and was
astounded at the vast number of fish that were caught
as a result. By obeying Jesus, Simon experienced the
power and wonder of God in his daily, working life.

We are called to listen to God's leading and obey
his will for our life. Our role model is Jesus, who
lived in perfect obedience to his Father, obedient
even to death on the cross. As he told his disciples,
love and obedience go hand in hand: 'If you keep my
commandments, you will abide in my love, just as I

have kept my Father's commandments and abide in his love' (John 15:10).

Since we're only human, there's bound to be a struggle when it comes to obeying God. Our vision of what God's will for us should be may be at odds with God's perfect understanding and knowledge of what's good for us. This can lead to disappointment that God's plan for us doesn't run parallel with what we've designed for ourselves. Obedience will lead to greater faith, a better understanding of God, and a deeper, closer walk with him.

PONDER

Do you find it hard to be obedient in practice, even if the theory is good?

Can you remember times when you have said 'no' or 'not yet' to God? What was the outcome?

How can you be more faithful in small, everyday matters, to help you when it comes to bigger things?

PRAYER

Loving Lord, you know the conflict that goes on in me sometimes, wanting my own way even if it clearly isn't your way. Help me to grow in obedience, I pray, and to embrace your loving purposes for my life.

Serving God and others

1

❁

The greatest commandment

"'You shall love the Lord your God with all your heart, and with all your soul, and with all your mind." This is the greatest and first commandment. And a second is like it: "You shall love your neighbour as yourself."'

Matthew 22:37-39

🌿

REFLECTION

Jesus has been asked what he regards to be the most important commandment in the Law and he quotes from the Old Testament books of Deuteronomy and Leviticus in his reply.

To love God goes beyond feelings to encompass our whole being. Our love for God springs from the love he has first shown us and includes surrender, obedience, commitment and service. We are commanded to be loyal and serve our King with an undivided devotion, living in such a way that no one and nothing else takes first place in our lives. Love and care of self must be healthy and God-centred, not self-centred. This involves how we regard parts of life that might threaten to take God's place, including material wealth, possessions, status, reputation, and other people. If our love for God is sincere, then our love and care for others will be equally genuine. We are called to put God's love into action, showing his love to the world. No one has ever loved God or others as perfectly as Jesus describes here. We inevitably fail to keep these commandments, and rely on the grace of God, not our own efforts, for our salvation and our place in the kingdom of God.

PONDER

Today, how have you obeyed God's call to love him and others?

Who is your neighbour?

Is it time to reassess some of your priorities?

PRAYER

Heavenly Father, I want to love you, and love and care for others, as I love and care for myself, and so fulfil your commandments. Forgive me when I fail and help me to do better, I pray.

2

❦

Loaves and fish

**There is a boy here who has five
barley loaves and two fish. But what
are they among so many people?**

John 6:9

🌾

REFLECTION

This is a verse from the familiar story of the seemingly
impossible task of feeding five thousand men, plus
women and children, as told in all four Gospel
narratives. The little boy gave what he had, Jesus
blessed the food and multiplied it, with the result that
there was much more left over at the end of the meal
(twelve full baskets) than at the beginning.

Even if it doesn't seem much to us, Jesus blesses
what we offer him and is able to multiply it. He can
take what appears to be inadequate or insignificant
and turn it into something that is not just sufficient
but abundant. Don't limit God by believing that what
you have to offer isn't good enough or that a situation
is impossible. The little boy's meagre contribution
made all the difference. If he'd been unwilling to

share his picnic, would the crowd have gone home hungry or would Jesus have had a plan B? When we are unwilling to offer what we have, other people may miss out. Remember that whatever we are able to give has come from God in the first place. If God asks us to do something, and we are willing, he will provide everything we need to do it. His power and resources are limitless, and miracles can happen!

PONDER

Consider what you have to offer God, in terms of your time, money, gifts and talents.

How have you helped to feed others today?

Look ahead to tomorrow and think how you can make yourself more available to God, in the small, everyday things of life.

PRAYER

God of miracles, when my offering
to you doesn't feel very important,
remind me of this story.
May I always be willing to share what
I have, for the benefit of others.

Treasure in jars of clay

**But we have this treasure in jars of
clay to show that this all-surpassing
power is from God and not from us.**

2 Corinthians 4:7 (NIV)

🌿

REFLECTION

It was usual in New Testament times for people to
hide their valuables for safe keeping in clay jars,
which had little value or beauty and wouldn't draw
attention to themselves or what they contained. Paul
speaks of Christian believers being like clay jars that
contain the precious gospel message of God's love and
salvation, a priceless treasure that has been entrusted
to them.

God has chosen to reveal his gospel message
through very ordinary people, like you and me. We
may feel that we are nothing special and are weak
and frail, fallible and vulnerable vessels. Our power
comes from God, who enables us to carry out his

work of sharing the gospel message in the world and letting people see the love of God through us. Our lives will shine with the 'treasure' that we share and will reflect God's glory and his love. God works with our strengths and our weaknesses and we must be in regular contact with him to maintain our source of power and strength. Paul acknowledges his own weakness, contrasting it with God's 'all-surpassing power'. Later in the same epistle (12:9), he goes on to record God's message to him: 'My grace is sufficient for you, for power is made perfect in weakness.'

PONDER

Reflect on this image of the clay jar and what it contains.

In what ways have you shared the gospel message with others today?

How could you shine more brightly for God?

PRAYER

All-powerful God, I may not feel very significant in the great scheme of things but thank you for entrusting your gospel message to me. Help me to share your love with the people I meet.

4

Developing a
servant heart

'So if I, your Lord and Teacher, have washed
your feet, you also ought to wash one another's
feet. For I have set you an example, that you
also should do as I have done to you.'

John 13:14, 15

REFLECTION

During the Last Supper, Jesus' final meal with his
disciples on the evening before his death, Jesus
performed the menial task of washing his disciples'
feet, a role usually allotted to the lowest servant. It's
a lesson in selfless, humble service and love, showing
the disciples that to be a leader they must develop a
servant heart towards each other and all people.

With Jesus as our role model, we are similarly
challenged to serve others, to make ourselves available,
to go the extra mile, to be there for others, alongside
them, paying attention, listening, offering friendship,
support and encouragement. It's all about the death
of ego and self-interest, and staying focused on the

greater goal, being prepared to serve in a way that brings glory to God, not to ourselves.

I recently read the account of one man's ongoing battle with cancer and was struck by the selfless attitude to life that shone through his words. Although deeply religious in his youth, he claims to have lost his faith on the death of his mother, some years before. Yet his philosophy, that he's here for others, not for himself, to make a difference and to help make the world a better place, is so profound and shows a true Christ-like, servant-heart attitude.

PONDER

Who have you been a friend to today?

If you are in a position of responsibility, how have you treated those who work under you?

Pray for more opportunities to be a servant to those God sends you to.

PRAYER

Teach me, good Lord, to serve you as you deserve, to give and not to count the cost, to fight and not to heed the wounds, to toil and not to seek for rest, to labour and not to ask for any reward, save that of knowing that I do your will.

(Saint Ignatius of Loyola)

5

❧

Sharing the good news

If I say, 'I will not mention him,
or speak any more in his name',
then within me there is something like
a burning fire shut up in my bones;
I am weary with holding it in, and I cannot.

Jeremiah 20:9

🌿

REFLECTION

The prophet Jeremiah had been faithful in proclaiming God's word but suffered only ridicule, mockery, insults and reproach from the people he addressed. While reluctant to carry on, he felt compelled to speak out and share God's message, regardless of the outcome.

If you feel reluctant and fearful when it comes to sharing the good news of the gospel, then relax because you are in good company. In the Old Testament there's a long list of people God chose to do his will but who were initially hesitant and full of fear. Think of Moses, for instance, who resorted to bargaining with God (see Exodus 3). These were 'ordinary' people but made great by God, who resourced them for the task in hand and moulded them into the kind of people he could use.

In the Temple, the prophet Isaiah heard God asking, 'Whom shall I send, and who will go for us?' He responded faithfully, 'Here am I; send me!' (Isaiah 6:8). God has a purpose for the situations he places us in, which may not be apparent at the time but becomes clearer with hindsight. If we make ourselves available, 'chance' meetings and conversations at just the right time may begin to take place.

PONDER

Are there times when you've felt God asking you to say or do something, but fear and reluctance have held you back?

Were you able to overcome those initial fears?

Have you felt drawn to a person or place 'at the right moment'? Do you think this is chance, coincidence or something more – a 'God-instance'?

PRAYER

Here I am, Lord, send me. Give me the courage to overcome my fear and reluctance, respond to your call and serve you faithfully in the everyday things of life.

6

❧

Fit to serve

**I can do all things through him
who strengthens me.**

Philippians 4:13

🌿

REFLECTION

Paul is confident that he can accomplish everything that God asks of him if he remains in union with Christ and relies on God's power and strength, not on his own limited resources. In 2 Corinthians Chapter 12, Paul acknowledges his own weakness, identified only as a 'thorn in the flesh', that kept him from pride in his own capabilities. Paul knows that even in his weakness, he can be strong in God's strength and grace. In his letter to the Ephesian Church (Chapter 6), Paul speaks of putting on the full armour of God, which is essential for complete protection in the spiritual battles we will face.

Pride might lead us to try and go it alone, to rely on our own energy and talents, believing that we can cope without God's help, especially in everyday, routine situations. However, if we are to achieve anything of lasting value in God's service, then we need every resource that God makes available to us. We have been called by God to serve him and need to be fit for that purpose. How can we hope to stand strong in our faith if our daily life does not include a prayerful putting on of God's armour for protection and acknowledging our need for God's power and strength? Fully equipped and prepared, we will be ready and able to serve God effectively.

PONDER

Can you recall those times during the day when you have most needed God's power, strength and protection?

How did you respond in those situations – by relying on God or on your own strength?

How can you prepare yourself better for the day ahead and whatever it may bring?

PRAYER

Almighty God, I recognise that without your strength in me, my efforts to serve you cannot fully succeed. Help me to lay aside my pride and lean more on you.

7

❦

Feed my sheep

**He tends his flock like a shepherd:
he gathers the lambs in his arms
and carries them close to his heart;
he gently leads those that have young.**

Isaiah 40:11 (NIV)

🌿

REFLECTION

The Prophet Isaiah's image portrays God as the Good Shepherd, who looks after his sheep with infinite loving care, guidance and protection, especially those who are most in need. At the end of John's Gospel, we read how Jesus reinstated Peter after his denial of Jesus before the crucifixion, instructing Peter to feed and take care of his sheep and lambs (John 21:15-17). God, in Jesus, is our perfect role model to imitate as he calls us, his followers, to take care of the 'sheep and lambs' he entrusts to us. The strength of our love for God and others will be revealed by how willing we are to serve God in this way.

In our daily life, being a good shepherd may mean simply being alongside someone who needs our help, empathising with them, trying to reflect God's unconditional love and compassion. Often there is no need to say anything much. Attempts at advice or wise words might seem hollow, like platitudes or clichés, if what the person really needs is a warm hug, or a friendly voice at the other end of the phone, ready to listen to them unjudgementally, reassuring them that they aren't alone with their problems. This is how we take care of God's 'sheep and lambs'.

PONDER

Can you look back and see times when God has positioned someone to be alongside you?

What qualities did you recognise in this person?

How have you been a good friend today?

PRAYER

Good Shepherd, as you have
loved and cared for me,
may I love and care for the sheep
and lambs you send my way.

8

❀

Stewards of God's world

'Be fruitful and multiply, and fill the earth and
subdue it; and have dominion over the fish of
the sea and over the birds of the air and over
every living thing that moves upon the earth.'

Genesis 1:28

🌿

REFLECTION

The creation of humanity was the climax of God's
creative activity. We are made in the image of
God, in his likeness, not with a physical resemblance
to God, but in personality, to be an extension of God,
to represent him and fulfil a crucial part of his work in
this world. God has ultimate control over the earth and
as part of creation, we are subject to the authority of our
Creator. But human beings have been given sovereignty,
as God's representatives, the right to 'rule over' the rest
of creation with the same loving care that God shows.

Dominion involves exercising stewardship over
creation on God's behalf. The privilege of humanity's

'kingship' in this world brought with it the responsibility of sharing God's work on earth and was never meant to be a domination that exploited the rest of creation. We are meant to care for the world and keep it as God created it to be. Creation was never intended to be solely for our benefit. We were made to be part of nature, not above it, and we need the rest of nature in order to survive, just as creation depends on us. Yet it often seems that Genesis 1:28 has been treated as a mandate from God to exploit the world's resources and animal life.

PONDER

How aware of 'green issues' have you been today?

In what ways could you be more involved in looking after the earth in your everyday life?

Are past attitudes to our planet, based on a misinterpretation of the biblical creation story, partly to blame for the current ecological crisis?

PRAYER

Creator God, you made all things well, but often we have not looked after the earth with loving care. Show me what more I can do to be a faithful steward of your world.

Becoming more like Jesus

1

❀

Being content

I have learned to be content whatever the circumstances. I know what it is to be in need, and I know what it is to have plenty. I have learned the secret of being content in any and every situation, whether well fed or hungry, whether living in plenty or in want.

Philippians 4:11, 12 (NIV)

🌿

REFLECTION

The Apostle Paul had learned a crucial lesson. He was able to see what was important in life from God's perspective. Paul focused on the eternal, drew on Christ's power for strength and relied on God's promises. His priorities in life were good, and he had a grateful, thankful heart.

Our acquisitive, consumer-driven society encourages us to desire more 'stuff', in the mistaken belief that material wealth can bring lasting happiness, security, fulfilment and contentment. Like Paul, we can resolve the tension between what the world presents as success and the call to follow God's way instead. We learn to cherish and be content with what we have, in whatever circumstances we may find ourselves, rather than wanting more, wishing life was different, better in some way.

Instead of fixating on what you haven't got, and feel is essential to your future well-being, focus on all the things God has already given you, and be thankful. It could be the time you have, your talents and gifts, your family and friends, or your job. The German word for feeling contented is 'zufrieden', meaning literally 'at peace'. We are offered God's peace and contentment, not fleetingly, as the world gives, but for all eternity.

PONDER

Are you discontented because you don't have something you earnestly desire? Consider whether this brings you into conflict with God's will for your life.

To what extent do you compare your life with other people's and find it wanting?

Can you be content with whatever God has in store for you?

PRAYER

God of peace, teach me how to be content,
like Paul, whatever life brings.
May I be filled to overflowing with your peace.

2

❦

Glad to be me

**Your beauty should not come from
outward adornment ... Rather it should
be that of your inner self, the unfading
beauty of a gentle and quiet spirit,
which is of great worth in God's sight.**

1 Peter 3:3, 4 (NIV)

🌿

REFLECTION

Peter's words are addressed to Christian wives,
encouraging them to focus on their inner beauty and
a spirit of godliness, instead of being overconcerned
with their outward appearance. Men and women
alike are created to be beautiful in God's sight. We
are made in his image, to reflect his glory. The world
tends to judge by outward appearance, whether
someone is easy on the eye, attractive and slim. Peer
pressure to wear the right designer labels and carry
the latest smartphone isn't limited to teenagers. If
current TV programmes are anything to go by, the
cult of celebrity and wealth is alive and well and
more popular than ever. But can adopting the world's

values ever make us truly contented and happy to be who we are?

There are some Christians, and you may be one of them, who are completely at ease with who they are, self-accepting and at home in their own skin. They know they are beautiful in God's sight, accepted and loved by him unconditionally, even though they are still a 'work in progress'. They are aware how God delights in them and God's spirit of joy within them is for all to see.

PONDER

Do you tend to be overcritical and only see your faults and flaws or are you happy with who you are?

Can you honestly say, 'Thank you, Father, for making me *me*'?

Over the course of the day, how have you let your beauty shine in the light of God's glory and power?

PRAYER

Loving God, I thank you that you look
at the heart, not at outward appearance,
and that you delight in me. May your
beauty be reflected in my life.

3

❀

Holiness

**As he who called you is holy, be holy
yourselves in all your conduct; for it is written,
'You shall be holy, for I am holy.'**

1 Peter 1:15, 16

🌿

REFLECTION

We should be holy, Peter writes, as our heavenly Father is holy. We are set apart and different from the world, in the sense that we belong to God and have dedicated our lives to him. A false idea of holiness is someone pious and saintly, withdrawn from the real world, who spends hours on end in prayer. When he was on the earth, Jesus went to quiet, remote places to be alone with his Father. Yet the Gospels also record how Jesus was totally involved with people and alongside them, building loving, practical relationships, the very opposite of being cut off and apart. He was the embodiment of the immanent holiness of God.

You may have spent time with people who make you feel better about yourself, and you come away more hopeful, with the world looking brighter. Such people don't make you feel inadequate or look down on you; quite the opposite, they affirm and encourage you. They point away from themselves to God and radiate his love and beauty. Being holy is about devoting ourselves to God, embracing his world and being involved in love and service. Fortunately, our holiness depends on God and his power, not on our own strength and resources.

PONDER

What do you think about God's call to be holy?

Have you met anyone today that you would call 'holy'? What was special about them?

How can you grow in holiness?

PRAYER

Holy Lord, teach me what it means
to be holy and set apart for you.
Let me look to Jesus,
my role model and guide.

4

❦

Patience

**Be still before the Lord,
and wait patiently for him.**

Psalm 37:7

❦

REFLECTION

Our world today is all about the instant and immediate, with no waiting. We have come to expect fast food, instant credit, mega-fast internet access . . . No end of TV advertisements tempt us with what we can have right now on credit, with no need to save up and wait. Don't worry now about how these goods will have to be paid for one day. Mobile phones can connect us in seconds with people across the world and there are apps for anything and everything imaginable. No wonder we have lost the patience to wait. If a train is late, or we're caught up in a traffic jam, we feel stressed and affronted that our journey will take longer than planned. We may have the latest in watches, with split-second accuracy, but we don't always have the time to wait patiently for something.

This impatience can find its way into our relationship with God, with instant answers to our prayers expected, rather than being willing to trust in God's timing. The cry may be: 'I need patience, Lord, and I need it *now*!' However, the fruit of the Spirit, which includes patience, takes time, possibly a lifetime, to grow and reach maturity in us. More important than learning to wait until what we want happens, is how our desires may change during the waiting.

PONDER

Are you waiting for an answer to prayer? How does that make you feel?

How highly do you rate patience as part of the fruit of the Spirit?

When you pray, do you expect instant answers or are you willing to wait and trust in God's timing?

PRAYER

Lord God, may I be more
open to your Holy Spirit.
Grow in me the fruit of patience
and help me to put my trust in you.

5

Words

**Let the words of my mouth and
the meditation of my heart
be acceptable to you, O Lord,
my rock and my redeemer.**

Psalm 19:14

REFLECTION

King David looked for God's approval for his words
and thoughts, as if they were praise-offerings that he
brought to the altar in the Temple.

Words have great power – they can be beneficial,
used to encourage and build up, or weapons that
criticise and destroy. Words may be spoken in
kindness, love and truth or be negative and false,
causing great harm. They can be faithful to God's
Word and glorify him, bringing blessing to others,
or threaten to undermine God's work in the world.
We may also speak negative, critical things about
ourselves that are destructive for our relationship with
God and other people.

In Chapter 3 of his letter, James warns about the power of the tongue, how it is impossible to tame, comparing the damage an uncontrolled tongue can do with a rampant wildfire. We should be careful what we say, and think before we speak. Writing to the Colossians, Paul says: 'Let your speech always be gracious, seasoned with salt, so that you may know how you ought to answer everyone' (Colossians 4:6).

PONDER

Think about how much God's love has guided what you have said today.

Do you need to ask God's forgiveness for any uncharitable, negative or unhelpful words?

Pray for anyone you have hurt by your words and ask for God's help to repair any damage to your relationship with that person.

PRAYER

Dear Lord, may I choose my words
carefully, so that they don't spill
thoughtlessly out of my mouth.
May my words bring honour
and glory to you.

6

Being pruned

**Every branch that bears fruit he
prunes to make it bear more fruit.**

John 15:2

REFLECTION

God is the divine gardener, Jesus is the vine and we,
as his followers, are branches on the vine. It is the
Father's will that we should bear fruit that is plentiful
and lasting (John 15:16), so branches that are already
fruitful are cut back to produce even more fruit.
This pruning process can be radical and painful at
times, and not what we might choose for ourselves.
Nevertheless, we are to be open to the pruning and
recognise that this time of purifying and cleansing
has a divine purpose. God is clearing away the dead
wood ready for new growth and fruitfulness, so we
can move forward with him.

Pruning may manifest itself in a time of discipline
that makes us stronger in our faith. God's discipline is
always for our well-being and is evidence that we are
his children, infinitely loved and cared for. Sometimes

God will allow us to endure difficult circumstances and times of trial, which are hard to bear and may seem pointless. As the writer of Hebrews says, discipline that is painful at the time, eventually 'yields the peaceful fruit of righteousness to those who have been trained by it' (Hebrews 12:11).

PONDER

How do you respond to God's discipline?

Are you open or resistant to God's pruning process?

Can you look back at difficult times and see their benefit in terms of increased fruitfulness in your spiritual life?

PRAYER

Heavenly Father, pain and hard
times aren't something I would
choose for myself, but I recognise
their long-term value in teaching me
to be more like your Son.
Help me to be more accepting
of your will for me.

7

❀

Failure

**Then Peter remembered what Jesus had said:
'Before the cock crows, you will deny me three
times.' And he went out and wept bitterly.**

Matthew 26:75

🌿

REFLECTION

Peter's previous rash but sincere promise to follow
Jesus anywhere and do anything he asked, looked
worthless in the light of his denial of Jesus. The
Bible records that many great men and women of
faith failed God at times, but he didn't give up on
them, which should encourage us. God chose people
who could be changed and transformed by his love,
and who would serve him faithfully, regardless of
their faults and failures. At the end of John's Gospel,
we read how Jesus reinstated Peter and the Bible
tells how Peter went on to do wonderful things in
God's service.

When we fail, there is always the possibility of
forgiveness. It's all part of our learning process, as we
grow more like Jesus. As a small child needs to be

helped up after stumbling and falling, we are lifted back up onto our feet, dusted down and shown loving care, not criticism and judgement. God forgives us when we turn to him sincerely, but it may be harder to forgive ourselves. We need to acknowledge our failure, accept God's forgiveness, let go of the regret and remorse and begin again.

PONDER

Do you feel that you've failed God in some way today and would like to turn back the clock to put it right?

Do you find it difficult to forgive yourself?

Focus on the difference between Peter, who was reinstated and Judas, who took his own life.

PRAYER

God of mercy and grace,
I thank you for your loving-kindness
and forgiveness.
When I let you down,
you are always ready to give me another chance.
Show me how to forgive myself too.

Positive thinking

Whatever is true, whatever is honourable, whatever is just, whatever is pure, whatever is pleasing, whatever is commendable, if there is any excellence and if there is anything worthy of praise, think about these things.

Philippians 4:8

REFLECTION

Paul encouraged his readers to focus their minds on good things, and to be positive, for whatever someone allows to occupy their mind, will ultimately influence what they say and do. Negative attitudes can come between us and God and harm our relationship with him.

Watching the daily TV news bulletins, there don't seem to be many reasons to be cheerful and positive, and there's a danger of being swamped by constant bad news stories. Often one dreadful story follows another and it's easy to adopt a negative, pessimistic mindset, concluding that nothing will ever change for the better. People are very good at complaining and grumbling, even if it's chiefly about the weather (if they're British) and such negative thinking can be very draining.

However, by focusing our minds instead on some of the qualities Paul listed and lifting our hearts to God in praise and worship, counting our blessings, it's possible to be more positive in everyday life. With a thankful heart, we remember God's love and his goodness. This is not simply adopting a blinkered approach to life, trying to be optimistic, regardless of circumstances.

PONDER

Resolve to begin tomorrow with praise and thanksgiving to God on your lips, even before you climb out of bed.

Start a list of things you can be thankful for, both small and big blessings, and add to it day by day.

How can you protect your mind from negative thoughts?

PRAYER

Father God, it's so easy to look down
at the ground and see only dust and dirt.
Teach me to look up to you and allow more
of your light and glory to be reflected in me.

SECTION 6

Words of encouragement

Into the sheer silence of the night
whisper words of comfort from the heart of God,
weaving a rich tapestry of love around me,
soft and warm like a blanket,
bringing rest to my soul:

You are my precious child and
all my love goes out to you.
Do not be afraid;
see, I have engraved you on the palms of my hands,
I will never forget or forsake you.

At last I will lie down and sleep in peace,
for you alone, O Lord, make me dwell
in safety and confident trust.

(Reference: Psalm 4, Isaiah 49:15, 16)

In the shadow of your wings
my soul has found true rest,
safe within your love I dwell;
you shelter me from harm,
protect me in the storm,
in the shadow of your wings, my peace.

(Reference: Psalm 61:4, Psalm 62:1, Psalm 91:4)

I have loved you with an everlasting love,
guarded you, the apple of my eye;
drawn you with cords of loving-kindness,
I have loved you with an everlasting love.

(Reference: Deuteronomy 32:10, Jeremiah 31:3, Hosea 11:4

Be still at heart, my child,
and let your striving cease,
in quietness and rest find strength;
like petals on a flower
let my plans for you unfold,
entrust to me your hopes and dreams.

(Reference: Isaiah 30:15)

3'Minute Prayers...

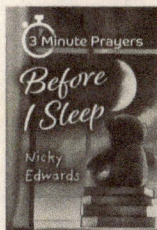

Before I Sleep
1501601

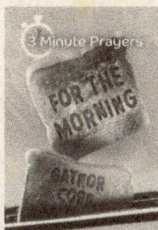

For the Morning
1501603

For the Weekend
1501604

For Coffee Breaks
1501605

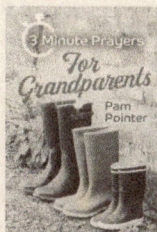

For Grandparents
1501606

www.kevinmayhew.com